Max the
Detective

Tony Bradman ■ Jonatronix

In this story

Max

Tiger

Mr Foster,
the caretaker

Mrs Mills,
the head teacher

One morning before school, Max and Tiger were in the playground. "Want to play football?" asked Tiger. "No thanks. I'm reading my book," said Max.

Max's book was about a detective.
"I want to be a detective when
I *grow* up," said Max.

grɔw

SPLASH!

Just then, Max heard a loud splash.
Tiger's football had landed in a
big puddle. That was odd. It had not
rained for days.

At lunchtime, Max went to wash his hands. That was odd. There was only a dribble of water in the taps.

Mrs Mills rushed by as Max walked
to the playground.
"There is a flood in the staffroom,"
she said, "I must find Mr Foster."

"A flood!" said Max, "Where has the water come from?" He went out into the playground. The puddle was getting bigger and bigger.

There was no water in some places and too much in others!
What was going on?

Maybe if Max was small he could find out! He pushed the button on his watch.

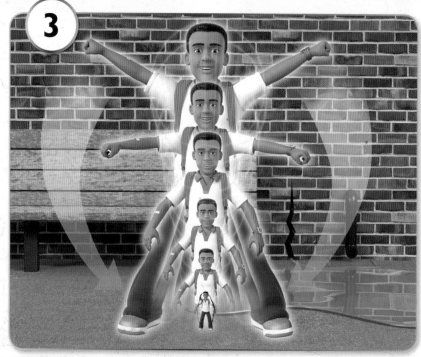

Now Max was small he could see
a crack in the wall near the drain.
He squeezed through it.

Max went into the crack and walked
along in the dark. There was lots of
water on the ground. He walked
along the tunnel.

Then he went round a corner
and saw the problem.

There was a hole in the water pipe! Water was leaking out. That was why there was a puddle in the playground! It was why there was no water in the tap.

"What a waste of water!" Max said. If the pipe was fixed, all the other problems would be solved.

How could Max fix it? He looked around him. There was nothing he could do. Unless …

Max took something from his bag.
He had a plan!

Max put his plan into action.
He put a sticking plaster over the
hole. The water stopped leaking.
"Problem solved!" he said.

Max walked back to the playground.
He pushed the button on his watch.

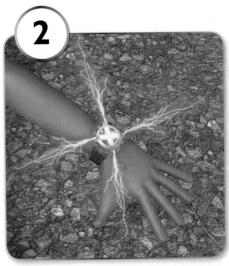

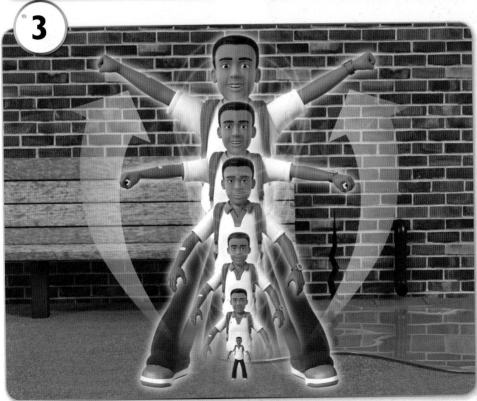

Just then, Max bumped into
Mr Foster.
"The taps are not working, there
is a flood and now this puddle,"
said Mr Foster. "I must try and
solve the problem!"

Max the detective said nothing.
He was looking forward to solving
his next case.

Later that day

Find out more

Read about Mr Big's new things ...

... and when Cat and Tiger fell in the bin!